ALDO LEOPOLD

Living With the Land

ALDO LEOPOLD

Living With the Land

Julie Dunlap

Illustrated by Antonio Castro

Twenty-First Century Books

A Division of Henry Holt and Company

New York

Acknowledgments

The author gratefully acknowledges permission to quote from the following: *The River of the Mother of God and Other Essays*, Susan Lader and J. Baird Callicott, eds, and *Aldo Leopold: His Life and Work*, by Curt Meine, published by the University of Wisconsin Press; and *A Sand County Almanac and Sketches Here and There*, by Aldo Leopold, published by Oxford University Press.

Twenty-First Century Books
A Division of Henry Holt and Company, Inc.
115 West 18th Street
New York, NY 10011

Henry Holt® and colophon are registered trademarks of
Henry Holt and Company, Inc.
Publishers since 1866

Library of Congress Cataloging-in-Publication Data
Dunlap, Julie.
Aldo Leopold : living with the land / Julie Dunlap
Illustrated by Antonio Castro. — 1st ed.
p. cm. — (Earth keepers)
Includes index.
Summary: A biography of the American naturalist who was a leader
in wildlife conservation.
1. Leopold, Aldo, 1886–1948—Juvenile literature. 2. Naturalists—
Wisconsin—Biography—Juvenile literature. [1. Leopold, Aldo,
1886–1948. 2. Naturalists.] I. Castro, Antonio, 1941-   ill.
II. title.   III. Series
QH31.L618D86 1993
333.95′16′092—dc20 [B] 93–1369 CIP AC
ISBN 0-8050-2501-4
First Edition—1993

Printed in Mexico
All first editions are printed on acid-free paper ∞.
10 9 8 7 6 5 4 3 2 1

Contents

"Conservation is a protest against destructive land use."

Chapter 1

Great Possessions

Another blizzard gripped Wisconsin in February 1935. A sharp wind was blowing snow into deep drifts, and most people were content to stay inside their warm homes.

But one family was out in the storm. A slim, gray-haired man strode through the snow ahead of his wife and five children. Aldo Leopold could not wait to show his family their new farm on the Wisconsin River.

When they reached the farm, however, the tired family could not share Leopold's excitement. To them, the land looked desolate. The cold wind rattled dry weeds standing in the old cornfield. Tree stumps stuck through the snow where the last owner had stripped the land of timber. "As far as the eye could see," remembered Leopold's daughter Nina, "was corn stubble, cockleburs, broken fences, and blowing sand and snow." And, instead of a cozy farmhouse, the only shelter they found was a chicken coop waist deep in frozen manure.

Leopold knew that his 80-acre farm had been abused and abandoned by its last owner. But unlike his family, he could see beyond the damage. Looking at the barren land, Leopold imagined a time when tall pine trees towered above February snowdrifts. One hundred years ago, he knew, this land was rich with birds and other wildlife. Perhaps one day, long ago, a wolf had padded softly through the fragrant, snowy pine forest.

At age 48, Leopold understood more about wildlife and wildland than almost anyone else. As a boy in Iowa, he had explored the forests and marshes surrounding his home. He had studied forests, prairies, and farmlands—and the animals that live there—as a forester and wildlife scientist for over 25 years.

He was now a professor at the University of Wisconsin and a pioneer in the new science of ecology, which is the study of living things in their environments. Ecology, Leopold often told his students, shows that land is a community. Each member of the community—including wildlife, plants, soil, water, and humans—depends on the others for survival.

Few people, Leopold believed, yet understood the message of ecology. His farm was just one example of how humans damage the land on which they depend, and Leopold knew of many other cases of destruction. He had seen marshes drained to grow corn, grasslands trampled by livestock, and forests stripped for lumber. "During my lifetime," Leopold wrote, "more land has been destroyed or damaged than ever before in recorded history."

"Conservation is a protest against destructive land use," said Leopold. He wanted to discover a way in which people could live without damaging the ecological community. By planting trees, wildflowers, and prairie grasses at his farm, Leopold hoped his family could re-create a "semi-wild" place where wildlife and people could thrive together.

In the spring after their first icy visit, the family pitched in to restore the farm. Everyone worked hard to plant trees and flowers and to turn the chicken coop into a cabin. But they also had fun. The children swam in the Wisconsin River and watched geese splashing in the marsh. At day's end, parents and children sang around the campfire. The whole family soon shared Leopold's joy in caring for the farm and his sense of belonging to the land community.

The book he wrote about his experiences at the farm, *A Sand County Almanac,* has inspired many people to change how they think about nature. In his *Almanac,* Leopold urged people to stop seeing land as property. "We abuse land," he explained, "because we regard it as a commodity belonging to us." Leopold wrote that land has beauty and value far greater than its worth in lumber, crops, or dollars.

The *Almanac* teaches that conservation is possible only when people change their attitudes toward nature. Leopold encouraged his readers to see themselves as members of the ecological community. When a person feels part of the land, Leopold believed, he or she will develop a sense of personal responsibility for its protection.

Leopold's writings have taught many people to see that the best way to stop environmental destruction is to change public values. Teaching values is now a basic part of environmental education.

Leopold knew that attitude change is possible. His own values had changed greatly during his years of studying and enjoying nature. Aldo Leopold's understanding of his place in the ecological community was "the end-result of a life-journey," a journey that taught him how "to live by and with, rather than on, the American land."

"I am glad I shall never be young without wild country to be young in."

Chapter 2

Built on Honor to Endure

Carl Leopold's shovel sliced into the cool earth. Clara, Carl's wife, placed an oak sapling into the new hole. The Leopolds were planting the tree to honor their new baby, Aldo, born January 11, 1887. Aldo's tree grew in front of the three-story house where he lived with his parents and grandparents in Burlington, Iowa. The house stood high on a bluff overlooking the Mississippi River.

From their windows, the Leopolds could see the railroad bridge that linked Burlington to Chicago and the eastern United States. Every day, train whistles signaled the arrival of new settlers from the East. Many were farmers, coming to plow Iowa's last acres of tallgrass prairie.

While the trains brought more people, the river carried logs that farmers needed to build new barns and fences. The timber had been cut from the vast pine forests of

Wisconsin and Minnesota, where lumbermen were chopping down trees so fast that logs sometimes jammed the Mississippi. Steamboats pushed rafts of pines down the river to Burlington's lumber mills. The saws that turned logs into lumber often whined from dawn until dusk.

Yet wildlands still surrounded the noisy city. Owls hooted in the wooded hills near Aldo's home. Across the river, a broad marsh was filled with the sounds of croaking frogs and, sometimes, the splash of a beaver's tail. Long after Aldo left Burlington, he remembered exploring his hometown's woods and marshes. "I am glad," he later wrote, "I shall never be young without wild country to be young in."

Aldo's parents were cousins, both children of German immigrants. Aldo's father grew up west of Burlington in the rough frontier town of Liberty, Missouri. Eight-year-old Carl was playing in Liberty on February 15, 1866, when Jesse James galloped into town to rob the bank.

The tall prairie grasses near Liberty were home to many kinds of wildlife, and young Carl roamed the rolling hills searching for birds' nests and fox tracks. He often carried a gun to shoot wild turkeys and rabbits for family dinners. For Carl, hunting the abundant wildlife was part of the great adventure of living in the wilderness.

Carl Leopold left Liberty as a teenager to live with his wealthy Uncle Starker in Burlington. There in the house overlooking the Mississippi, he met his cousin Clara, who shared his passion for the outdoors.

Besides being a champion ice skater, Clara loved to

garden. She and her father planted trees and flowers, turning their yard into a neighborhood park. One day, a newspaper reporter passed by. In an article for the Burlington *Hawkeye*, he called the park a "bird's paradise."

Carl and Clara were married in 1886. The Leopolds planted a tree for each of their four children. After Aldo came his sister, Marie, his first brother, Carl, Jr., and finally his baby brother, Frederic. While Clara took care of the children, Carl Leopold ran the family business. The Leopold Desk Company built fine rolltop desks from cherry, oak, and walnut trees. Carl regularly inspected his factory, checking each desk to be sure its craftsmanship lived up to his business motto, "Built on Honor to Endure."

Growing up in the Iowa countryside, the children found that each season had its own adventures. On some winter nights, Aldo and Carl, Jr., climbed to the roof of the house for starlight snowball fights. On icy mornings, Clara taught the children how to skate on the Mississippi.

When it was too cold to play outside, Aldo curled up next to his dog, Spud, to read. One favorite story told the adventures of a fierce wolf called Lobo living in the rugged mountains of New Mexico. As he read and reread the story, Aldo longed to see the wildland where Lobo had lived.

Winter's highlight came at Christmas. Smells of spicy holiday cakes filled the Leopold house. A ceiling-high fir tree shimmered with glass ornaments and candles. Dozens of mirrors decorated the walls, and Aldo watched the dancing candlelight while the family sang German Christmas carols.

In spring, Aldo's father drove the family in a wagon for picnics in the woods. On walks after lunch, Carl Leopold shared his joy in nature with Aldo. Carl showed his curious son where to find a mink's den in a hollow tree and how to learn from a pile of droppings what a raccoon had eaten for dinner. Carl's discoveries awakened Aldo to the delights of studying the animal world.

Aldo waited impatiently for the family's annual vacation. The Leopolds and their dogs spent every summer at Les Cheneaux Club on an isolated island in Lake Huron. After a short train ride to Chicago, the family boarded a steamship to cross Lake Michigan. They finished the trip to Les Cheneaux Club in a smaller boat. The 24-hour voyage always made Aldo seasick, but he calmed his stomach by nibbling on hard, dry biscuits brought for the dogs.

Other vacationers at the club relaxed by playing golf or chatting with friends. But Aldo rowed through the island's creeks and bays, fishing for trout and pike. Early one morning, after a long struggle, he landed a huge northern pike weighing 15 pounds. He also joined family camping trips to the Canadian mainland. The dense forest was the wildest country Aldo had yet explored. At night by the fire, he dreamed of paddling a canoe deep into the unknown land. Aldo later wrote, "Every youth needs an occasional wilderness trip, in order to learn the meaning of this particular freedom."

School had already started by the time the family returned to Burlington each fall. Aldo was a serious student, and his fascination with nature shone through all of his schoolwork. One English composition described the 39 kinds of birds he had observed in his yard. "I like wrens," wrote 11-year-old Aldo, "because they do more good than almost any other bird, they sing sweetly, they are pretty, and very tame."

Aldo was shy and made few school friends. His one close friend was Edwin Hunger, the local paper boy. On foot, the pair searched the autumn countryside for birds. Aldo always carried a notebook, and he showed Edwin how to sketch the birds they found. Edwin later remembered Aldo as "the finest and truest friend I've ever had."

For Aldo, the highlight of the fall was hunting with his father. Each autumn, millions of ducks and geese followed the Mississippi River south from their northern nesting grounds toward warm winter territories. Many migrating birds stopped to rest and feed in the marshes across from Burlington. On brisk Saturday mornings, father and son rose before dawn and headed for their favorite hunting spot—Eagle Swamp. They sat under a tree, gnawing on bread crusts and waiting for ducks. One snowy Saturday, Aldo waited all afternoon, "growing colder with each passing crow." He never forgot shooting his first duck that day at sunset.

From his father, Aldo learned that killing was not the reason for the hunt. Carl Leopold taught his son that hunting was a special way to feel close to nature. On fall hunting trips, Aldo learned to feel part of the natural rhythm of bird migrations.

As Aldo was growing up, he and his father noticed that fewer migrating birds passed Burlington each year. Professional hunters throughout the country were killing millions of ducks, geese, and other birds to sell in markets and restaurants. Few laws existed to limit the killing because most people in the 1890s believed that the tremendous flocks were inexhaustible. Dead birds were sold by the wagonload.

Alarmed by the shrinking flocks, Carl Leopold decided to limit his own hunting. He shot fewer birds of all kinds and stopped killing any rare birds. Aldo followed his father's example. For the rest of his life, Aldo Leopold admired his father for taking personal responsibility to help solve the problem.

In the late nineteenth century, prairie grasslands were also rapidly disappearing. They were being destroyed to grow crops and to feed cattle. And the great northern pine forests were vanishing. From his house on the bluff, Aldo could see that fewer pine rafts floated down the Mississippi each year.

A few people were beginning to protest against environmental destruction. Theodore Roosevelt, who became president in 1901, was the leader of a new movement to conserve the country's wildlife, forests, and grasslands for public use. "These resources," Roosevelt said, "must be preserved for future generations to use and to enjoy."

Theodore Roosevelt's ideas excited Aldo. At 16, he announced to his parents that he wanted to follow a career in forest conservation. To do this, Aldo knew he had to go to college. His mother convinced him that he should

prepare by finishing high school at the respected
Lawrenceville School in Lawrenceville, New Jersey.

A few days before his seventeenth birthday, Aldo arrived at Lawrenceville. It was the first time he had been separated from his close family. He took breaks from his studies to write letters home about his classes and the birds he was seeing on hikes through nearby farmland.

One letter from his family in 1904 described the continuing slaughter of migrating ducks. Aldo's response showed his sadness at the loss. He promised his parents that he would work hard to protect the birds "when my time comes to have something to say."

Chapter 3

Scientific Forestry

Aldo soon got a chance to speak out against forest destruction. Students at the Lawrenceville School gave public speeches each year, and in December 1904, it was Aldo's turn to talk. He told his audience that the nation's forests were vanishing. "The lumber supply of our country," he warned, "is now almost used up."

In his speech, Aldo blamed the forest decline on wasteful logging practices. Lumbermen in the 1800s, Aldo explained, treated the forests as if they were endless. Using a practice called clear-cutting, loggers cut down all of the trees in one area even though they used only the largest and finest. When they moved on to a new forest, Aldo said, the loggers left behind acres of dead trees and brush. The debris often caught fire. Fire and logging destroyed the plant roots holding the forest soil, and the dirt soon washed away in the rain. Aldo told his listeners, "Where was yesterday a bountiful land, is today a barren, lifeless waste."

Aldo asked in his speech, "How can this useless destruction be prevented?" Growing numbers of Americans were asking that same question. The United States government owned millions of acres of forest land. Some people wanted to preserve the public forests by creating parks and forest reserves where logging would be banned.

The leader of the fight for preservation was the environmentalist John Muir. In articles and books, Muir criticized loggers because they destroyed the beauty of wild places. People need beauty, Muir wrote, as much as they need lumber.

Other Americans, however, opposed closing any public forests to logging. President Roosevelt's adviser on conservation was Gifford Pinchot. He believed that forest resources—grass, soil, water, and minerals, as well as trees—should be used by the public.

According to Pinchot, the way to protect public forests was to learn how to use the resources without damaging the land. Forest scientists in France and Germany, where Pinchot had studied, were developing new methods to grow trees like crops. By cutting trees with less waste and replanting, forests could be used now and in the future,

Pinchot said. He wanted these scientific management techniques to be practiced in American forests, so that forests would be conserved through "wise use."

President Roosevelt agreed with Pinchot. In 1905, Roosevelt put Pinchot in charge of managing 86 million acres of public forest. As Chief of the United States Forest Service, Gifford Pinchot needed trained foresters to help him control the use of forests throughout the country.

Aldo was eager to study forest management. As a forester, he thought, he could work outdoors, studying and enjoying nature while helping to prevent forest destruction. In 1905, the only school in the country that trained professional foresters was Yale University's Forest School. The Forest School accepted only college graduates, so Aldo enrolled in college at Yale's Sheffield Scientific School.

In September 1905, Aldo arrived in New Haven, Connecticut, to begin his studies. Like the Sheffield School's other pre-forestry students, Aldo took difficult courses in science and mathematics.

He studied hard, but he also took time to explore the Connecticut countryside. At least once a week, Aldo rode a trolley to the edge of town and hiked into the woods. East Rock, Pine Rock, and Maltby Lakes were only a few of the new places he discovered for hiking and studying birds.

Aldo's parents wrote often. Some of Carl Leopold's letters described his work to help establish Iowa's first hunting laws. Aldo's father and other people who hunted waterfowl for sport wanted laws to protect the flocks from destruction by market hunters. To control the killing, sport hunters in Iowa and throughout the country were fighting for laws limiting the number of birds each person could kill in one day. Carl Leopold's work for wildlife laws gave Aldo another reason to admire him. Years later, Aldo praised his father as a "pioneer sportsman."

Clara Leopold's letters encouraged her shy son to make college friends. Aldo surprised her—and himself— by joining Yale's debating society and by training for the track team. He even joined his friends in cheering at the Yale football games.

One of his favorite companions, however, was not a college friend but a New Haven boy named Benjamin Jacobosky. Bennie had grown up in a tough city neighborhood, and Aldo enjoyed taking Bennie on his first trips into the woods. With fishing poles in hand, the pair tramped along twisted stream banks far from the noisy city. Bennie's excitement on each trip reminded Aldo that every child needs wild places to explore.

Whether hiking or studying in New Haven, Aldo looked forward to his vacations in Burlington. He wrote home about his plans to go "a-blackberrying" and "a-picnicking" and to enjoy "cutting the fresh grass and a whole million other delights, all included in 'summer.'"

On one vacation, however, Aldo observed changes in the land near his hometown. He discovered sadly that his favorite marsh had been drained and planted with corn. "The job was so complete," he later wrote, "that I could not even trace the outlines of my beloved lakes and sloughs under their new blanket of cornstalks." Aldo felt the loss for the rest of his life. He said, "Perhaps no one but a hunter can understand how intense an affection a boy can feel for a piece of marsh."

In 1907, he was too busy to visit Burlington on summer vacation. Instead, Aldo and his classmates spent the summer studying at the Forest School camp in Milford, Pennsylvania. Yale professors at the camp gave the future foresters their first lessons in the techniques of conserving the forest for use. Through lectures and fieldwork, Aldo learned the three main steps of forest management: inventory the existing trees, harvest logs with limited waste, and grow new trees for future use.

Aldo's professors explained that foresters must inventory a forest—identify, count, and measure the trees—to know how much timber can be harvested from one area. Pacing through a forest to calculate the harvest is called "timber cruising."

In a 40-acre forest plot, Aldo practiced identifying the types of trees that people want for lumber, such as white pine. He counted and measured a sample of trees to estimate the number and size of each type on the plot. Aldo neatly recorded his estimates in a small notebook. The smell of pines surrounded him while he used his notes to calculate the amount of usable lumber in the plot.

To harvest trees with little waste, the students learned the technique of "selective logging." One professor, carrying an ax, led Aldo's class through the woods. First, the teacher marked each pine big enough to cut. Next, he skillfully chopped one down, demonstrating how to knock down one tree without damaging its neighbors. Selective logging, he said, reduces the number of trees killed by loggers. Also, because no unused, dead trees are left on the ground, the technique helps prevent the fires that kill young trees and increase erosion. By logging selectively, foresters usually leave young trees to grow for future harvesting.

Another way to grow new trees is to transplant tree seedlings. Aldo enjoyed digging in the cool forest soil, planting straight rows of young pines. His professor reminded him, though, that planting is just the first step in growing new trees. The seedlings must be protected from many kinds of damage, such as grazing animals. Growing a new, healthy forest, Aldo's professor said, takes many years of hard work.

Aldo had plenty of hard work to do when he returned to New Haven. He took classes to sharpen his skills in identifying trees and mapping forest land. In one class, he learned more about the U.S. Forest Service. The service now managed over 150 million acres of national forest. Some of the wildest public lands were in Arizona and New Mexico territories, where loggers had not yet harvested the mountain forests. Aldo remembered reading about the adventures of a wolf in the southwest, and he imagined cruising the timber in the unspoiled forests.

For their final training, the young foresters traveled by ship to another forest camp in Texas. The men spent

long, hot days measuring trees in the swampy cypress forests. One evening, a tired Aldo wrote home complaining of the mosquitoes and snakes. His mood improved, though, when a package of gingerbread arrived from his mother.

Despite the difficulties, Aldo loved the hard work and rough living. His training as a forester was giving him the skill to manage forests wisely and the opportunity to work outdoors. One night by the campfire, he wrote home about his forestry work. "If you could see the full moon tonight, sailing high over the towering pine-trees, you would like it, too. I have decided, again and again, that it is worth all the trouble."

Another night, the young foresters sat by the campfire, talking about their future plans. Most were joining the U.S. Forest Service, but they did not yet know where they would be working. After a hot day in Texas, one man wanted to manage a cold forest in Minnesota. Another longed to harvest California's giant redwoods. Aldo, though, talked of the wild Southwest and said, "That is where I want to go."

*"Natural resources are
interdependent."*

Chapter 4

Wise Use

On July 18, 1909, Aldo Leopold stepped off a stage coach in Springerville, Arizona Territory. The cool mountain breeze felt refreshing after his two-day ride from the desert below. Covered with dust from his trip, the 22-year-old forester was eager to begin his first job with the U.S. Forest Service.

In Springerville, Forest Assistant Leopold reported to the headquarters of the Apache National Forest. Over one million acres in size, the Apache was a wildland of rich variety. A forest of ponderosa pines covered the White Mountains, and cottonwood trees lined the canyons of the Blue Range. On the plains and high plateaus grew lush meadows of grasses and wildflowers. The Apache's forests and grasslands were home to antelopes, mountain sheep, golden eagles, and wolves.

The Apache was established in 1908 to manage the

use of its abundant natural resources. Although few settlers had yet braved the rugged land, demand for its resources was increasing. New copper mines south of the Apache needed lumber to prop up their tunnels, and growing herds of cattle and sheep grazed on the Apache's ranges.

The Forest Service encouraged the use of trees and grass on the Apache, but foresters feared that too many livestock could destroy the forests and grasslands. Chief Forester Gifford Pinchot had studied the effects of heavy grazing and observed that livestock eat and trample tree seedlings and grasses. Where plants are destroyed, rains wash away the soil, preventing future growth.

Pinchot concluded that overgrazing wastes plant and soil resources. He decided that the Forest Service should require ranchers to buy grazing permits, limiting the number of animals each rancher could pasture in one area. Controlling the number of grazing animals, Pinchot believed, is an important part of conserving national forests through wise use.

Leopold's first job was to help manage the forests that would supply timber for local copper mines. The Forest Supervisor needed an inventory of the amount, location, and kinds of trees near the mines. Leopold's boss gave him a five-man crew and orders to inventory the forest, or cruise the timber, in the Blue Range. Riding a horse named Jiminy Hicks, Leopold led his crew of timber cruisers into the mountains. Each morning, the cruisers hiked out of camp to survey 40-acre plots of the wild forest.

It was tough work. Day after day, the men struggled up and down steep slopes in the hot sun. Leopold's sweaty fingers sometimes smudged his careful notes. His skin smarted from the bites of deer flies and the scratches of locust thorns. Often, too, food supplies ran low. Leopold had to interrupt his work to hunt deer for his hungry crew.

One afternoon, Leopold and another timber cruiser stopped to rest on the rim of a canyon. They spotted a pack of wolves crossing the river below. Foresters, including Leopold, blamed wolves for killing livestock and deer in national forests. Gifford Pinchot encouraged his men to shoot wolves and other predators on sight.

Leopold and his companion grabbed their rifles and blasted at the animals. The pack scattered, leaving behind only one wounded female. The men clambered down the rocks. "We reached the old wolf in time," he later wrote, "to watch a fierce green fire dying in her eyes." That day, Leopold believed that killing predators was good for the

forest. As Leopold later explained, "Everyone assumed that the fewer varmints the better." But the memory of the wolf's dying eyes would haunt him for years to come.

Snow was falling in the mountain passes by the time the cruisers rode back into Springerville. Leopold spent the winter in town, using the inventory notes to write a plan for harvesting the timber.

In the spring of 1910, Leopold got his first chance to help manage grasslands. Ranchers were driving sheep and cattle to high pastures for the summer, and the Forest Supervisor needed to limit the number of livestock to prevent overgrazing. Leopold rode to the Apache's scattered ranches and pastures, checking grazing permits and counting stock. After traveling hundreds of hot, dusty miles, Leopold called that spring "the outworkin'est time I've had so far."

In 1911, Leopold's concern about grassland conservation deepened when he was transferred to the Carson National Forest in New Mexico Territory. Riding across the Carson's mountains and high plateaus, he saw that the land was damaged by severe overgrazing. Livestock herds had destroyed grasses and tree seedlings in many places. Erosion gullies cut into the hills, and the eroded dirt muddied the Rio Grande and other rivers. Leopold feared that wasteful grazing practices were ruining the Carson's resources.

Unlike the Apache, the Carson Forest had been heavily grazed for generations. Leopold and other Carson foresters thought that lowering the number of grazing animals would stop the range damage. In time, they believed, the grasslands would recover. Leopold wrote a plan to reduce the size of livestock herds. Foresters worried that ranchers would fight the changes, but Leopold vowed to enforce the reforms "if it takes a sixshooter to do it." Fortunately, the ranchers cooperated.

Leopold was not always counting trees or managing grasslands. One night at a party, he danced with 20-year-old Estella Bergere. Estella's Spanish ancestors had raised sheep near the Rio Grande for over a century. Leopold visited her often at her family's hacienda, or ranch, and the couple were married in Santa Fe, New Mexico, on October 9, 1912.

A few months after the wedding, Leopold almost died of kidney failure. His doctor expected him to recover slowly, if at all. Estella took him home to Burlington, where he spent his days in the house overlooking the Mississippi. The rest gave him time to read the latest books on conservation. One new book, *Our Vanishing Wild Life*, revived Leopold's interest in wildlife conservation. The author, William Temple Hornaday, warned that wild animals were headed for extinction. "It is necessary to sound a loud alarm," Hornaday wrote, "for otherwise it will be too late."

Leopold had recovered enough by the fall of 1913 to celebrate the birth of his first son, Starker. The young family returned to New Mexico, although Leopold was still too weak to work. When his father died the next year, he made a brief, sad trip back to Burlington to attend Carl Leopold's funeral.

Aldo returned to work in 1914 with a renewed commitment to wildlife conservation. He was alarmed that antelope, mountain sheep, and other game (wild animals hunted for sport) were becoming scarce in southwestern national forests. The Forest Service did not yet manage wildlife because wild animals were not seen as valuable forest resources. The animals' only protection was a few, rarely enforced state game laws. As a forester and a hunter, Leopold believed that game should be used more wisely.

Leopold's boss, Arthur Ringland, was also concerned about game conservation. Ringland asked Leopold to convince local foresters and hunters to help solve the problem.

For his fellow foresters, Leopold wrote a detailed handbook about game in the southwest. Wildlife, he argued, are valuable forest resources to be conserved for future use. He encouraged foresters to enforce state hunting laws because hunters need game, just as ranchers need grasslands.

To educate hunters, Leopold gave speeches on game conservation throughout New Mexico and Arizona. He urged hunters to support stronger laws that would limit hunting and to take personal responsibility for obeying hunting laws.

Aldo Leopold was praised widely for his work to conserve national forest game. One day, he opened a letter of congratulations from Theodore Roosevelt, who thanked him for "setting an example to the whole country."

In 1919, Leopold's conservation concerns broadened when the Forest Service promoted him to Chief of Operations for New Mexico and Arizona. Leopold became responsible for inspecting the management of 20 million acres of national forest.

One inspection tour in 1921 took Leopold back to the Apache National Forest. Riding ranges he had last seen in 1911, Leopold was alarmed by the damage livestock had done to the land. The high meadows were split by erosion gullies too wide for his horse to jump. In the mountain valleys, his horse scrambled over rocks where floods had washed away trees along with the soil. Leopold's eyes stung from eroded dust carried by the wind.

The Apache trip was a turning point for Leopold. Witnessing the damage taught him that land use could cause soil loss even when the Forest Service controlled grazing. He saw clearly that grass and forest resources would be lost if foresters did not learn how to protect the soil. "Natural resources are interdependent," Leopold wrote. To protect the grass and the forests, forest scientists must discover how to save "that fundamental resource, land."

Leopold experimented with ways to prevent soil loss. In one study, he found that planting trees along streams slowed stream-bank erosion. But he could not find a way to stop all land damage caused by grazing or other uses.

A few undamaged areas remained in wild, remote parts of the national forests. New roads, though, were bringing new users. Leopold feared that the last wilderness would disappear. He wondered if saving the last wild places from damaging uses could be a "wise use" of the land.

Saving wilderness, Leopold knew, was a controversial idea. Gifford Pinchot and other foresters believed that all the public lands should be open for controlled resource use. However, John Muir and other environmentalists argued that the wildest, most beautiful parts of the country should be preserved from any human use. For a time, Leopold felt torn between Pinchot's idea of conserving land *for* use and Muir's idea of preserving land *from* use.

At last, he thought of a solution. Leopold believed that people could hunt or hike in a wilderness without causing damage. The Forest Service, he decided, should save wilderness areas for use in public recreation. In a 1921 article for the *Journal of Forestry*, Leopold challenged the Forest Service to protect wilderness. He defined "wilderness" as "country preserved in its natural state, open to lawful hunting and fishing, big enough to absorb a two weeks' pack trip," without roads, buildings, or "other works of man."

There was only one place left in the southwest big enough and wild enough to match Leopold's definition—an isolated section of the Gila National Forest in New Mexico. He proposed that the Forest Service protect the region as the Gila Wilderness Area.

As Leopold expected, other foresters attacked his proposal. His opponents said that the public would lose money if the Gila's timber and other resources were not used. Leopold replied that the Gila's resources were too difficult to reach to be worth much anyway.

More important, Leopold argued, wilderness has a

value greater than money. He explained that exploring wild country filled him with a sense of freedom and possibility. All Americans, he firmly believed, deserved opportunities for such adventures. Leopold told other foresters that wilderness should be preserved "for the spiritual and physical welfare of future Americans, even at the cost of acquiring a few less millions of wealth."

Because of Leopold's persistent efforts, the Forest Service created the Gila Wilderness Area on June 3, 1924. Leopold rejoiced. For the first time, Aldo said, foresters had looked at wildlands and declared, "This is wilderness, and wilderness it shall remain."

"The time has come for science to busy itself with the earth itself."

Chapter 5

Science in the Wild

Ten-year-old Starker Leopold joined his father on a wilderness trip in June 1924. For 14 days, they paddled their canoe through the cold rivers of Minnesota's Superior National Forest. One day, Starker caught three trout for dinner. That night by the campfire, Aldo wrote in his journal, "The number of adventures awaiting us in this blessed country seems without end."

By this time, Aldo and Estella had three sons and a daughter—Starker, Luna, Carl, and Nina. After the June trip, new adventures were awaiting the Leopolds. The family moved to Madison, Wisconsin, where Leopold began a new job at the U.S. Forest Products Laboratory.

The laboratory was the center for Forest Service research on the use of wood to make paper and building materials. Leopold's scientific interests had grown during his experiments on soil erosion in New Mexico, and he wanted to learn more about research techniques from the forest scientists at the laboratory. However, Leopold's boss kept him busy writing reports instead of doing experiments. Leopold walked quickly home each afternoon, eager to take his family exploring.

Madison, Wisconsin, in 1924 was a compact city, surrounded by farms, lakes, and marshes. On many evenings, the Leopolds bicycled to Lake Mendota. On weekends, the family hiked along the Wisconsin River bluffs. Leopold listened for geese and told stories about the huge flocks he saw as a child.

The family, however, did not find wilderness near Madison. The great northern forests that Leopold had read about in high school had been cut down. Left behind was a region of brush and stumps called "the cutover." Wisconsin's last wild prairies and marshes were being replaced by farm fields. And as the wilderness disappeared, waterfowl and other wildlife populations shrank.

Aldo was especially concerned about the waterfowl decline, a continuing national problem. Conservationists fought over how to solve it. One group of concerned hunters wanted farmers to stop destroying the wetlands that the birds need for feeding and nesting. Another group, led by William Temple Hornaday, blamed hunters for killing too many birds and argued for stronger hunting laws.

Neither group, Leopold suspected, knew enough about waterfowl to understand the problem. "It is amazing how little is known," he wrote. While the two sides quarreled, bird populations dwindled.

Leopold thought that field research on wild game populations would help conservationists decide what to do. He could not study game, however, while working at the Forest Products Laboratory. After four years at the laboratory, Leopold resigned from the U.S. Forest Service.

An organization of gun manufacturers agreed to pay Leopold for an eight-state study of game populations. In July 1928, he left Wisconsin on his first research trip. He drove to meet conservation experts in Michigan, who alerted him that quail were getting scarce. As a hunter, Leopold knew that quail usually live in overgrown edges around farm fields. Michigan's farmers, however, were plowing their brushy edges to plant larger crops. Walking through their neatly planted fields, Leopold saw that farmers were destroying the habitats needed by quail.

Each state he studied had different game problems. In Wisconsin, he found that both hunting and wetland drainage were reducing waterfowl numbers. Leopold made lists of the many factors limiting different game populations, including hunting, predators, disease, and habitat loss. For most game, predators seemed to pose a smaller problem than Leopold had expected. The evidence was growing, however, that habitat destruction was the biggest problem.

On a research trip to Iowa in 1928, Leopold met a game researcher named Herbert Stoddard, who described his experiments to improve quail habitat. Through test plantings, Stoddard explained, he had discovered plants that quail need for food and shelter. When he grew the plants on farms, quail populations increased. The work reminded Leopold of forest scientists' efforts to manage forest growth. He realized that Stoddard was a pioneer in a new science—game management.

Leopold felt the science of game management could be used to combat the destructive effects of farming on game populations. In early 1929, he decided to write a book for conservationists about managing game through habitat improvement. The gun manufacturers he worked for agreed to pay him while he wrote.

A few months after he started to write, the U.S. economy collapsed. When the Great Depression began, tens of thousands of people lost their jobs. Many banks and factories closed, but the gun companies Leopold worked for were still in business. He worked steadily on his book, trying not to worry about losing his job.

One Sunday in 1931, Leopold took a day off to look for a new local hunting spot. Near Riley, Wisconsin, he met a farmer named Reuben Paulson. The men soon discovered they shared "an incurable interest in all wild things, great and small, shootable and non-shootable." Paulson complained, though, that he found little game on his land. Leopold offered to help improve the habitat in exchange for permission to hunt on the farm. Working with Paulson, Leopold turned the farm into a laboratory for testing his management ideas.

As the Great Depression worsened in the early 1930s, the gun companies warned Leopold that they could not support him much longer. He wrote quickly on pads of yellow paper, and his children (except little Estella, born in 1927) took turns typing the manuscript. Thanks to everyone's efforts, the book was almost complete when his salary stopped in 1932.

Game Management was published in 1933. In the book, Leopold argues that game management science should be used both to prevent and to repair damage to wildlife populations. For waterfowl, for example, preventing marsh drainage is an important management technique. To increase quail numbers, however, managers can replant edge habitat. Leopold urged farmers, especially, to learn management techniques and use them on their land.

Managing game was important to Leopold because, he believed, wildlife is useful and beautiful. He still saw game as a valuable resource for hunters, and one of his goals was to grow "crops of wild game for recreational use." But he also valued wildlife as a beautiful part of wild nature. He criticized farmers and other land users who destroy wildlife habitat to make more money. "Are we too poor in purse or spirit," he wrote during the Great Depression, "to keep the land pleasant to see, and good to live in?" To Leopold, management science was a way to balance the beauty and usefulness of the land.

Conservationists praised *Game Management*, but few practiced Aldo's techniques during the depression. Conservation was viewed as a luxury in hard economic times.

Leopold was still unemployed. The family lived off savings inherited from Leopold's father, and they felt lucky compared to many neighbors. Wisconsin's farmers, especially, were suffering from the depression and a lack of rain. As the drought dried up their crops, winds blew away the soil. Native grasses had protected the soil during previous droughts, but farmers had plowed the prairies

and marshes. When the eroded fields could no longer support crops, many farmers abandoned their damaged land.

Concerns about the state's farmland and wildlife led the University of Wisconsin to create a new faculty position in the College of Agricultural Economics. In June 1933, the university offered the job to Leopold, by now a national expert on erosion control and wildlife management. He happily accepted, proud to become the country's first professor of game management.

At first, Professor Leopold did little teaching. The university president asked him to help plan a new arboretum. Usually, an arboretum is a museum-like place where trees are displayed and studied. Leopold and the other planners, however, wanted something "new and different." Instead of a collection of trees, they envisioned recreating prairies, forests, and wetlands that had existed when Wisconsin's first European settlers arrived. The planners hoped the arboretum would restore "a sample of original Wisconsin."

Rebuilding native landscapes, Leopold knew, would be more complex than improving habitat for a few game species. The university wanted to restore whole natural communities, including many species of plants and animals, as well as the soil they lived on. Game management techniques could not do the job.

Leopold and other arboretum scientists needed a new science—ecology. Ecology is the study of living things in relation to their environment. In the 1930s, ecologists were just beginning to understand the complex network of relationships in natural communities. An understanding of natural relationships was the key to creating the arboretum, Leopold felt.

To restore prairies and forests, ecologists needed

places where they could study what plants and animals lived in native communities and to find native seeds, plants, and wildlife. Fortunately, a few acres still existed that farmers had not yet plowed or loggers had not yet cut. Leopold saw that these small wild places had great scientific value. Protecting wilderness gained new importance for him. Only on wildland could scientists discover how natural communities functioned before they were damaged by humans.

Damage to the land caused a national crisis in 1934. Farming and overgrazing had destroyed native grasslands throughout the Midwest, and a severe drought was withering the crops. On May 9, a windstorm swept across the dry farmlands of the Great Plains and carried away tons of soil. Dust clogged the air, choking people and animals caught outside. The May storm was the first of many that created an agricultural wasteland known as the "Dust Bowl."

Five weeks after the first storm, Leopold spoke at the opening ceremony of the arboretum. "Ecology," he began, "tells us that no animal—not even man—can be regarded as independent of his environment." When humans abuse the land, they are forgetting that "plants, animals, men, and soil are a community of interdependent parts." He told the audience that humans must learn to cooperate with the rest of the environmental community.

Leopold criticized scientists, in particular, for inventing machines to "exploit and enslave the earth." Instead, he argued, scientists should study natural communities and experiment with restoring damaged land. Leopold paused and looked at the crowd. "The time has come for science to busy itself with the earth itself."

*"If education does not
teach us these things, then
what is education for?"*

Chapter 6

An Ecological Education

Nina Leopold placed a pine seedling in the new hole in the sandy ground. Nina's father, leaning on his shovel, wrote neatly in a small notebook: 2,000 pines planted in April 1936.

Aldo Leopold's notebook recorded the details of a new experiment. He and his family were working to restore one of the many Wisconsin farms abandoned during the depression. The Leopold farm was 50 miles north of their home in Madison, in a flat, sandy part of Wisconsin called "the sand counties." As on many neighboring farms, the soil was eroding after years of wasteful farming techniques. Most of the trees had been cut for timber. During recent droughts, fires had scorched the marsh and burned the farmhouse to the ground. As Nina Leopold later remembered, the land "had been carelessly lumbered, carelessly farmed, and carelessly abandoned."

The farm restoration differed from the arboretum project. Arboretum researchers were restoring landscapes that existed before settlers lived there. The Leopolds, however, were working to create a weekend home, a place to live simply and enjoy the wildness around them.

The family's first chore at the farm was to turn the old chicken coop into sleeping quarters. Aldo, Starker, and Luna shoveled out the manure, and everyone helped build a fireplace. Instead of buying lumber to make benches and tables, Leopold looked for boards washed up on his land by the Wisconsin River. Once straw mattresses were dragged inside, "the shack" was ready for weekend planting trips.

Besides pine trees, the Leopolds planted berry bushes, tamarack trees, and patches of grain for wildlife food and shelter. Nine-year-old Estella carried buckets of water to the trees, but as the drought continued, nearly all the pines were dead by summer. Leopold wrote the bad news in his journal, but the family refused to be discouraged. They made plans to try again next spring.

Back in Madison, Leopold was busy teaching at the University of Wisconsin. Students came from all over the country to study game management with him. With a smile, Leopold welcomed them to the new profession of "wild-life management," as he now called his work. He urged each to share his enthusiasm for research. "The most fun lies in seeing and studying the unknown," he once said. The students warmed quickly to Leopold and soon awarded him a nickname he cherished, "The Professor."

Each student worked independently on a field project, and Leopold loved to visit their study sites. "In the field he really came alive," one student remembered. As Leopold examined a study site, he challenged the student

to study more than just a few game species. His excitement at finding skunk droppings, for example, showed Leopold's appreciation of the ecological importance of all wildlife. Although Leopold himself had once thought of skunks and other predators as useless or even harmful pests, he now taught students to see predators as another fascinating part of the environment. "When we attempt to say that an animal is 'useful,' 'ugly,' or 'cruel' we are failing to see it as part of the land."

Wisconsin's farmers also learned about conservation, thanks to Leopold. To combat the national soil erosion crisis, President Franklin Roosevelt created the Soil Erosion Service to train farmers how to stop damaging their land. Leopold helped convince the service to establish the nation's first erosion control demonstration farms in Wisconsin. Leopold called the farmer training project "an adventure in cooperative conservation" because the government worked with private landowners to prevent soil damage.

Leopold viewed damage prevention as just one part of farmland conservation. In talks on the university's radio station, he gave farmers ideas about how to improve their land. In one talk, he explained how to grow grape vines to attract quail. To Leopold, a farmer who both grew crops and created wildlife habitats practiced a "harmonious balanced system of land-use." That farmer's land, Leopold told his radio audience, would "tell a story of tolerance toward living things, and of skill in the greatest of all arts: how to use the earth without making it ugly."

The Leopolds spent their first Christmas at the shack in 1936. For four days, the family skied around the farm looking for deer tracks in the deep snow. They warmed up in the shack, eating hot sourdough bread baked over the fire. At night, parents and children sang Spanish folk songs around the fireplace. Leopold wrote in his notebook, "Too good a time to make note in journal."

Spring trips to the shack were now an annual ritual. Each year, Leopold dug more holes to plant more pines. Mrs. Leopold planted wildflowers and prairie grasses, and Starker grew grapes to feed quail. All of the children built birdhouses for purple martins and screech owls. But in the evening, planting and hammering stopped while the family listened to geese honking on the marsh.

Vandals broke into the shack in 1938, destroying most of the furniture and chopping the fireplace mantle with an ax. When the family discovered the destruction, everyone cried. "All, that is, but Dad," Nina Leopold remembered. "He just looked around, saw our state, and burst into a

big smile. 'I didn't know how much this place meant to you,' he said. 'Let's get busy.' "

Between repair trips, Leopold taught a new course in wildlife ecology. The class, open to all university students, allowed Leopold to share his joy in exploring nature with students who had never studied the land.

On field trips, Leopold told each student to bring only "eyes, ears, and notebook." The group often drove to a nearby farm, where Leopold asked questions that challenged students to observe and think. What birds should we see this morning? Why are some species missing? What could the farmer do to improve the land? On a field trip with Leopold, one friend remembered, "He'd stretch your brains until they were tired."

Through his questions, Leopold helped students understand their place in the environment. When a student sees land as a community, Leopold wrote, "He will see the beauty, as well as the utility, of the whole, and know the two cannot be separated. We love (and make intelligent use of) what we have learned to understand." His ecology class, he hoped, taught love and a feeling of responsibility for the land. "If education does not teach us these things, then what is education for?"

Leopold's teaching routine was broken in 1941 when the United States entered World War II. Since most of Leopold's students interrupted their studies to fight overseas, he had more time to write. A book on conservation could teach more people than he would ever meet in his classrooms. He decided to turn his journal about life at the shack into essays, explaining what he had learned about living with the land. Each weekday morning, Leopold woke before dawn and walked through Madison's quiet streets to his office. He sat down at his desk, pulled out a sharp pencil and a pad of paper, and began to write.

On weekends during the war, the Leopolds continued to visit the shack. Luna and Carl, however, had joined the military. The family worried especially about Carl, who was fighting in the Pacific. During one month, his location was a military secret. In a letter home, though, he described the local wild birds. Aldo studied the letter and exclaimed, "I know where Carl is!"

As the war dragged on, public interest in conservation dropped. Most people thought that supporting the war effort was more important. Few protested, for example, when logging increased in the national forests. But when the lumber industry threatened a Michigan wilderness, Leopold fought back.

He interrupted his book to give speeches and write letters urging protection of an ancient maple forest in Michigan's Porcupine Mountains. In an article for *Outdoor America*, Leopold explained the many values of the wilderness—for recreation, science, education, and beauty. If the wilderness were saved, he believed, these values could endure far longer than the war. Leopold cheered in 1943 when the Michigan legislature voted to declare the forest a state park.

After the war ended in 1945, Leopold's students hurried back to Madison. His sons had survived, and Leopold celebrated Carl's return by taking him hunting. On a crisp November morning, the men tramped through a local farm with guns on their shoulders. They spent the day searching for pheasants and admiring the golden needles on the tamarack trees. After hunting all day, Leopold noted in his journal, "Didn't fire a shot."

Aldo and Estella Leopold and their daughters shared the tenth spring planting trip in 1946. The family could see that their work had changed the land. Wildflowers bloomed in the small prairie they had planted. Thousands of pines had lived through the droughts, and now chickadees hopped in their branches. Quail nested among the grape vines.

Leopold thought happily of all that his family had learned and enjoyed at their sand country farm. "Decent land-use is worthwhile," he wrote, "not only for its effect on land, but for its effect on the owner."

After another round of planting, Leopold dedicated himself to finishing his book. Several publishers rejected the essay collection, fearing that it would not sell. But on April 14, 1948, an editor called, offering to publish *A Sand County Almanac*. Leopold was overjoyed. To celebrate the news, he packed up the car to take his wife and daughter Estella to the shack for a spring planting trip.

"When we see land as a community to which we belong, we may begin to use it with love and respect."

Chapter 7

A Sand County Almanac

Most almanacs are yearbooks, month-by-month guides to weather, tides, star movements, and other events. But Aldo Leopold had a different kind of almanac in mind. He wanted readers to use *A Sand County Almanac* as a guide for living with the land.

The book begins in January at the Leopolds' sand county farm, with stories describing "events in that cycle of beginnings and ceasings which we call a year." Leopold loved observing nature in January. "January observation," he wrote, "can be almost as simple and peaceful as snow, and almost as continuous as cold. There is time not only to see who has done what, but to speculate why."

One January morning, Leopold found skunk tracks in

deep snow. The footprints led him through the woods and across a meadow. As he followed, Leopold thought about the skunk. "I wonder what he has on his mind; what got him out of bed?"

Along the way, there were signs of other animals—nibbled oak seedlings where rabbits had passed, bits of fur where a hawk had caught a rabbit. Finally, the skunk tracks disappeared into a pile of driftwood. Was the skunk still inside? Leopold was content not to know; sometimes, he found mystery more exciting than answers. He turned happily homeward, "still wondering."

The first sign of spring at the shack was the arrival of migrating waterfowl. When the farm's wetlands thawed in March, tired geese would "tumble out of the sky like maple leaves." The sounds of their honking and splashing would carry across the farm, and the Leopolds would know, "Our geese are home again!"

The spring activities of another bird, the woodcock, were harder to detect. "I owned my farm for two years," Leopold admitted, "before learning that the sky dance is to be seen over my woods every evening in April and May." Male woodcocks call and dance at sunset, flying in spirals high into the sky. Since discovering the dramatic dance, Leopold wrote, "My family and I have been reluctant to miss even a single performance."

Yet Leopold knew most other farmers did not watch woodcocks. Such farmers, he believed, preferred sitting inside theaters to exploring their own land, searching for sky dancers. "They live on the land, but not by the land."

In summer, Leopold rose in the cool hours before dawn. He sat on a bench outside the shack, sipping coffee and recording in his journal the time each local bird gave its first song. Each call was full of information as well as beauty. Leopold understood that the "clear tenor chant" of the male field sparrow announced the bird's claim to a nesting territory. The morning filled with songs of robins, buntings, and wrens, each proclaiming possession of space. Their music told Leopold of all the creatures who shared his farm—in fact, who saw this land as their own.

In midsummer, Leopold celebrated a "prairie birthday." A "pin-point remnant" of native grassland still survived in the corner of a cemetery near his farm. He waited each July for the appearance of a few "saucer-sized yellow blooms" of a prairie flower named Silphium. Huge bison herds, Leopold imagined, had once grazed on Silphium meadows. To him, the plant was a "surviving celebrant" of the prairie wilderness.

Plowing and mowing by humans, however, were destroying Silphium. It had grown so rare that few people had seen it, or knew that it was disappearing. "We grieve only for what we know," Leopold wrote. "What a thousand acres of Silphium looked like when they tickled the bellies of the buffalo is a question never again to be answered, and perhaps not even asked."

By fall, Leopold needed a fire for warmth when he sat outside the shack on cool mornings. Few birds sing in autumn, but Leopold still listened. He wrote, "It is on some, but not all, of these misty autumn daybreaks that one may hear the chorus of the quail." The chance to hear a rare, unpredictable bird song was one of Leopold's joys at the farm. "We felt honored by this daybreak hymn sung almost at our doorstep."

In October, the leaves on the Leopolds' blackberry

bushes turned brilliant red. The leaves were "red lanterns," Leopold said, lighting his way on frosty morning hunts. Partridges sometimes hid among the blackberry briars by the creek, and he searched the banks with gun in hand. For Leopold, hunting was another way to participate in life on his farm. "There is value in any experience," he wrote, "that reminds us of our dependency on the soil-plant-animal-man food chain."

One Sunday in November, Leopold tracked a raccoon to its den in the roots of an upturned maple tree. Finding a wild animal's home in a dead tree gave Leopold another lesson in how plants and animals depend on one another. "Every farm is a textbook on animal ecology," he wrote. By living close to the land, Leopold and his family had learned how to read the book.

Snows blanketed the farm again in December. As the year came to an end, Leopold thought of the pines he had planted on the farm. Thousands now grew, straight and tall, to shelter wildlife and hold the sandy soil.

Yet Leopold knew that other people were destroying trees, meadows, and marshes on other land. "We still slip two steps backward for each forward stride," he wrote. Despite decades of conservation efforts by Leopold and others, people were still damaging the environment.

Leopold thought that he knew why. In the *Almanac's* final essay, "The Land Ethic," he explains that people abuse land when they see it only as a resource for making money. Farmers who want a larger crop to sell, for example, will plow bird habitat if all they care about is economics. The first step toward conservation, then, is to "quit thinking about decent land-use as solely an economic problem."

Instead, Leopold argued, people should see decent land use as a personal responsibility. This change can occur when people understand that they belong to an interdependent, ecological community. People who feel part of the land, like the Leopolds, will protect bird habitat for its beauty and ecological value, even if they could make money by destroying it.

Leopold wrote, "When we see land as a community to which we belong, we may begin to use it with love and respect." The idea that land is to be loved and respected, rather than used for pure profit, is the essence of Leopold's land ethic.

Can humans change the way they value and treat the land? Aldo Leopold thought so. He told the story in the *Almanac* about the day he shot a wolf in Arizona's Blue Range. In 1909, Leopold remembered, he killed a wolf because he wanted to protect game animals and livestock for human use. By 1948, Leopold understood that wolves are an important part of the natural community. He now believed that the mountain lost part of its wildness when the "fierce green fire" died in the wolf's eyes.

In his own lifetime, Leopold had changed from a forester who protected the economic values of natural resources into an ecologist who studied and loved the land as a whole. If he could change, other people could, too.

Chapter 8

The Land Ethic

Aldo Leopold did not live to see *A Sand County Almanac* in print. One morning during the family's 1948 spring planting trip, he saw smoke rising from a neighbor's fields. Leopold rushed to help battle the fire. Working at the edge of the blaze, he suffered a heart attack and died, at age 61, on April 21, 1948.

At his death, Leopold was already well known as a wilderness advocate, ecologist, and author of *Game Management*. The public bought few copies of his *Almanac* at first, but some conservationists recognized its importance. One predicted that the *Almanac* would be read "for decades, and probably centuries, to come."

Interest in *A Sand County Almanac* grew in the 1960s as concern for environmental problems deepened. In 1962, Rachel Carson's book *Silent Spring* alerted the public to the dangers of pesticides. Passage of the Wilderness Act in 1964 increased public awareness of the need to protect wildlands. The first paperback edition of the *Almanac* appeared in 1966, and sales jumped. As Leopold hoped, the book has helped him teach people a new way of seeing—and treating—the land.

The founder of Earth Day, Gaylord Nelson, is one of the many environmentalists who read and reread the *Almanac*. After wilderness activist David Brower read the book, he called Leopold "a friend I never met." Environmental historians agree that Leopold's *Almanac*, along with Rachel Carson's *Silent Spring* and Henry David Thoreau's *Walden*, is one of the most influential books in the American environmental movement.

What makes Leopold's book so powerful? Through stories about his life at the shack, Aldo Leopold shows that humans can live in harmony with the natural community. People can stop destructive land use if they learn, as Leopold did, to balance their own needs with those of wildlife, wilderness, and the land as a whole. "Harmony with land," Leopold wrote, "is like harmony with a friend; you cannot cherish his right hand and chop off his left."

Aldo Leopold is also remembered for his many other accomplishments. In 1954, the U.S. Forest Service erected a plaque honoring him at New Mexico's Gila Wilderness Area. Leopold has been called the "father of the national forest wilderness system" because of his work to protect the Gila and his writings on the values of wildlands. The Forest Service wilderness system now protects 33 million acres, and Leopold's writing still inspires wilderness activists who share his belief that "raw wilderness gives definition and meaning to the human enterprise."

Scientists, too, gain inspiration from Leopold's work. The University of Wisconsin Arboretum, where Leopold began restoring forest and prairie communities in the 1930s, is now a world-famous center for research in restoration ecology. William R. Jordan, III, an ecologist at the arboretum, calls the idea of restoring and studying native landscapes one of Leopold's most "far-reaching contributions to the modern conservation movement."

The Leopold family still owns their sand county farm. In cooperation with neighboring farmers, they have protected almost 1,400 acres as a wildlife reserve and research station called the Aldo Leopold Memorial Reserve. Children and adults alike are welcomed to the reserve, to help with the planting and to learn about Leopold's ideas of living with the land.

Near the end of his life, Leopold penciled a note explaining his goals in teaching the next generation of conservationists. He wanted each of his students to develop a "warm personal understanding of land," combining ecological knowledge with love and a sense of personal responsibility for the environment. Once an individual understands the land, Leopold wrote, "I have no fear of what you will do to it, or with it. And I know many pleasant things it will do to you."

Glossary

arboretum a place where many types of trees are shown and studied

almanac a book published yearly that contains useful information in many fields, such as calendars, holidays, and weather predictions

conservation the process by which natural resources are saved

cutover an area of brush and stumps that remain after a forest has been cut down

drought a long period with no rain

ecology the study of living things in relation to their environment

environment the physical world that surrounds a plant or animal

erosion the gradual wearing away of the earth's surface

game an animal that is hunted

habitat an area or environment in which a plant or animal normally lives

migration	the seasonal movement from one location to another
plateau	an elevated and level area of land
predator	an animal that survives by preying upon others
reserve	public land saved for a special purpose
resource	an available supply
sapling	a young tree
scientific management	using scientific principles and methods to care for and maintain something, such as a wildlife habitat
territory	an area of land
timber	trees thought of as a source of wood
timber cruising	to inventory a forest by identifying, counting, and measuring the trees
varmint	an animal or bird considered a pest
waterfowl	a bird that swims
wetlands	a moist lowland area, such as a marsh
wilderness	an area of land left in its natural state
wildlife	animals or plants living in a natural state

INDEX

N.E. TACOMA